The Pillow Story™
A Soft Little Fable

The Pillow Story™

A Soft Little Fable

Written by Rick Moser
Illustrated by Rex Bohn

The Pillow Story™

www.widespark.com

Published by WideSpark Design

14 N. First Ave, 2nd Flr

St. Charles, IL 60174 USA

ISBN: 978-0-578-03986-2

Made from Recycled Paper

In Dedication to Nicholas
and Emily and their
big brother Matthew

Once upon a time,
on a fall afternoon,
three geese huddle
with their flocks
as they often like to do.

There are blue geese in the north field, brown geese in the west and gray geese in the east.

They will all fly south in the frosty cold morning. Winter is coming. . .all the signs are here.

Three geese feel a bit restless though. . . for they hear a small voice whisper "go your own way."

They turn their heads around and feel the warmth of their flocks, yet listen to their hearts and take off into the night.

Though they are afraid, upward they fly, guided by the moonlight and a far twinkling star.

Suddenly, high in the sky,
the three strangers meet up. . .
and bump right into each other!

Honk, honk, honk!

"Hey, watch out!"

honks the first, a blue

one named Bluebelle.

"You too," honks the second, a grey one named Greyson.

"What are we doing here?" honks the third, a brown one named Woody.

After a bit more honking
they come to understand,
they've been called on a journey
to a place under the star.
Though of different colors
they move into one formation
in the geese V shape:
one in front, and two behind.

After flying towards the star
for who knows how very long
it shines its light downward
upon an old wooden barn.
    Their wings are tired of flapping
and their minds are tired too.
A drink of water and bed of straw
will do them so much good.

Inside they find a man
fast asleep in the straw.
His clothes are so old
and his body is so worn.

The three are cold and tired and also quite afraid, yet they take care of the man as if he were their own.

"Let's give him comfort,"
honked Bluebelle.

"Let's make him warm,"
honked Woody.

"Let's make him a pillow,"
honked Greyson.

So they found an old sack
which used to hold seed and
stuffed it with their feathers,
the softest they could find.

Then they put the comfy
pillow under the man's sleepy head,
and huddle in close so he is
safe and warm.

Then they said a prayer of thanks
for the man and the barn, and after
whispering "good night," fell into
a deep, deep, sleep.

Next morn they are awakened
by the sun's warm rays shining
through the windows onto
their golden webbed feet.

To their great surprise the
man and the pillow were gone!
They turned their heads around
yet he was nowhere to be found.

Where did the man go?

Where was the pillow they made for him?

Was it all a dream?

"Well, I hope he is safe,"
honked Woody.

"I hope he is warm,"
honked Greyson.

"I sure hope he took his pillow,"
honked Bluebelle.

So they waddled to the door
and honked around a bit more,
where on wooden pegs they found
three little vests filled with down!

These were special vests made of sack cloth and feathers. . .

each one sized just right
with a gold star stitched
right above the heart.

It was frosty cold that morning
in the high wintry air. . .

yet the feather vests
kept them warm along
with thoughts of the man.

So they turned their golden
beaks to the warm southern
sun and rose high into the sky
wings flapping, side by side.

"This man sure was special," honked Bluebelle. "I enjoyed giving him our feathers."

"This journey was special. I enjoyed getting to know you and working together," honked Greyson.

"This Pillow Story is special. Let's share it with our flocks when we get back home," honked Woody.

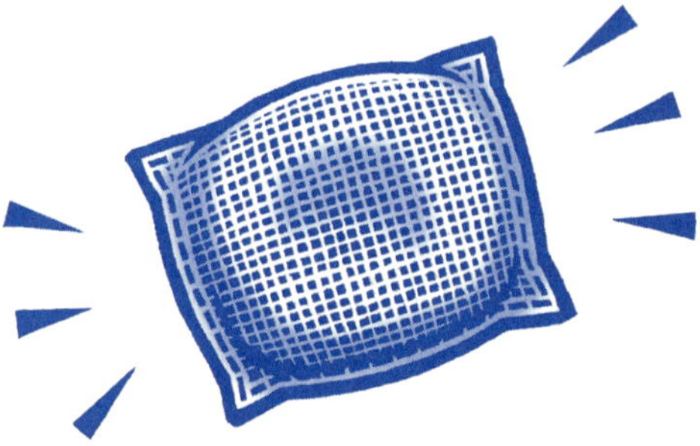

In their proud V shape they came to understand how much they have in common and how special was the man.

It was the softest little lesson they had ever felt.

Be true to your heart.

We are all the same color
on the inside.

Treat the least of your brothers
as the greatest.

Kindness is never wasted.

We are stronger together.

The End

Pillow Storytime Discussion Questions

1. Do you like to look at stars at night?
   What is your favorite?

2. Have you ever been away from your family?
   How did it make you feel?

3. Do you have any friends who are "of different color"?

4. Have you ever seen a homeless person?
   How did it make you feel?

5. Do you have a down coat or vest?

6. How do you think the three vests got there?

7. What is something you'd like to tell a friend about *The Pillow Story*?

Have a great answer you'd like to share? Visit **www.pillowstory.net** and click on Share Your Comments at the bottom.

Lazarus House

Five U.S. dollars from the sale of each copy in the first printing of *The Pillow Story* is donated to Lazarus House in St. Charles, Illinois, USA. Lazarus House is an emergency shelter, transitional living facility and homeless prevention outreach program. Their mission is to provide hospitality, safe shelter, nourishing food and support services for those in need, in order to help them retain or regain successful, independent living. Their first donation was from a ten year old child who asked her friends to bring money for the homeless to her birthday party, rather than gifts. From that humble beginning in 1997, Lazarus House has expanded to serve thosands of people, providing hope and a hand up. . .not a hand out.

For more information about Lazarus House visit www.lazarushouseonline.com.

Lazarus House
ST. CHARLES FREE
METHODIST CHURCH
214

"What a beautiful story! As children grow to find their place in the world, this fable is sure to help bring about important discussions of acceptance. I am certain to read it to my students for many years to come."
-Mary Kartheiser, Elementary School Teacher

"Whenever children see and hear geese fly over the fields, *The Pillow Story* will come to mind. A delightful little story with a great moral."
-Frances Gustafson, School Teacher (retired)

"Lazarus House is very grateful to Rick Moser for his gift of *The Pillow Story*, which so beautifully describes what we should all be about: caring for those in need with love, compassion and dignity. May all who read this story be blessed by it and determined to live out its lessons."
-Darlene Marcusson, Executive Director,
Lazarus House

My sincere thank you to:

Aesop

Jim Aalfs

Holly and Mary Charles Ambrose

Ann Barta

Kerri Cordray

Betty and John Cragan

Frances Gustafson

Jack Harries

Ben Joyce

Rosemary Kesse

Carsten Martensen S.J.

Mary Meyer

Dave Moravec

George and Mary Moser

Susan Richards

Susan Scott

Dr. Jaena Stanley-Gonzaga

David Starke

Cindy Vincent

Gary Wright

Maryanne Vandenbergh

RM